Contents

This daily prayer book is a prayer book designed to be prayers for all people, past present and future.

This prayer book is designed for all people who would like to pray morning, afternoon and evening on a daily basis, whether you attend services anywhere or not.

There are many people around the world who do not have access to attend services for all types of reasons.

This is why I have created and published this book.

I originally just wanted to create a book to use that was not bulky,

that was condensed and had all or almost all of the prayers that I say daily because I was always having to change the pronouns etc..

in what I was reading to say my prayers to be inclusive of others.

I truly believe that everyone should not only pray for themselves but also for all people and souls from the beginning of time to eternity.

I feel like if we pray this way we are praying for all the loved ones that came before us and will come after us. I am not perfect and this book is not perfect but it is my desire that all people should be able to afford a prayer book.

Another reason for this book is the internet is not always available for everyone, as well as I would rather be holding a physical copy of a lightweight book that I can use no matter where I am at without being on the internet.

Daily Blessings

Morning Blessings

When we first wake up.

We give thanks before You
eternal and living King

who returns our souls within
us with mercy.

Great is Your faithfulness.

Washing hands

Blessed are You, Lord our God,
King of the universe,

Who has made us holy through
His commandments,

and has commanded us
about washing hands.

Bodily Functions Blessing

Blessed are You, Lord our God, King of the universe,

Who created mankind with wisdom, and created within

us various openings and cavities. It is obvious and known

before Your Heavenly Throne that should any of them

become obstructed or should any of them break open, it

would be impossible to remain alive even for a short while.

Blessed are You, Adonai, Who heals all flesh and does

wonderous things.

Morning Blessings Continued

Our God, the souls You have placed within us is pure.

You created them, You fashioned them. You breathed

them into us. You safeguard them within us, and

eventually You will take them from us and restore them

to us in Time To Come.

We gratefully thank you from the beginning through

eternity for not only ourselves but for those that came

before us, and present and come

after us, Lord, our God,

Master and creator of all
works, Lord of all souls.

Blessed are You, LORD, who
restores souls to all.

Blessed are You, Adonai, our God, King of the universe,

Who gives the rooster the
understanding

to distinguish between day and night;

Who gives sight to the blind;

Who releases those who are bound;

Who stands upright those
who are bent over;

Who clothes the naked;

Who gives strength to the weary;

Who spreads the earth over the waters;

Who provides for the footsteps of man;

Who has provided us with
all our needs;

Who girds Israel with might;

Who crowns Israel with splendor;

Who did not make us gentles;

Who did not make us slaves;

Who makes us according to his will;

Who removes the bonds of

sleep from our eyes,
and slumber from our eyelids;

May it be Your will, Adonai, our
God, God of our forefathers,
that You accustom us to Your
Torah and make us cleave to
Your commandments.

Do not bring us to sin;

to iniquity;

to be tested;

to shame;

to evil;

Please spare us;

from the impudent;

from impudence;

from evil in any shape or form;

from anyone or thing that is bad;

from any mishap;

from slanderous talk;

false testimony;

from hatred in any form;

from libel;

from unusual death;

from the 1st death;

from the 2nd death;

from illness;

from harmful occurrences;

from litigation;

and from a troublesome adversary
and adversaries-whether

he, she, they be a Jew or not
a Jew and from the

judgment of Gehinnom.

Blessed are You, Adonai, our God, King of the universe,

Who has sanctified us with
His commandments, and

has commanded us concerning
the words of the Torah.

Make the teachings of Your Torah, Adonai, pleasant in

our mouths and in the mouths of Your nation, the House

of Israel. May we and our children, and the children of

our children, past, present and future, all of us be those

who know Your name and study Your Torah for its own

sake. Blessed are You, Adonai, Who teaches Torah to

His people Israel.

Blessed are You, Adonai, our God, King of the universe,

Who chose us from among all the nations, and gave us

His Torah. Blessed are You,

Adonai, Who gives the Torah.

Adonai spoke to Moshe, saying:

Speak to Aaron and his sons, saying:
So shall you bless the children

of Israel – say to them: "May Adonai
bless you and watch over you.

May Adonai illuminate His
countenance for you and
be gracious to you.

May Adonai turn His countenance
toward you and establish peace for

you." They shall place My Name
upon the children of Israel,

and I will bless them.

Shema

Hear, O Israel: Adonai is our God,
Adonai is One! Blessed is God's name;
His glorious kingdom is
for ever and ever!
And you shall love Adonai your God
with all your heart, with all your soul,
and with all your might.
And these words which I command
you this day shall be upon your heart;
teach them faithfully to your
children, speak of them in your
home and on your way, when you
lie down and when you rise up.
Bind them as a sign upon your hand;
let them be a symbol before your eyes.
Inscribe them on the doorposts of
your house and on your gates.

For Healing

Give ear, Adonai, to our prayer, heed our plea for mercy.

In time of trouble we call to You, for You will answer us.

When pain and fatigue are our companions, let there be

room in our heart for strength. When days and nights

are filled with darkness, let the light of courage find its

place. Help us to endure the suffering and dissolve the

fear. Renew within us the calm spirit of peace.

Blessed are You, Adonai,

Healer of the Sick.

Afternoon Blessings

Psalm 23

Adonai is my shepherd;

I shall not want.

He makes me lie down in
green pastures;

He leads me beside the still waters;

He restores my soul.

He guides me in straight paths
for His name's sake.

Yea, though I walk through the
valley of the shadow of death,

I shall fear no evil, for You are with me.

Your rod and Your staff--
they comfort me.

You have prepared a table before me

in the presence of my enemies.

You have anointed my head
with oil; my cup overflows.

Surely goodness and mercy shall
follow me all the days of my life,

and I shall dwell in the house
of the Lord forever.

Psalm 121

I lift up my eyes to the mountains;

What is the source of my help?

My help comes from Adonai,

Maker of heaven and earth.

God will not let your foot give way;

your Guardian will not slumber.

Behold! The Guardian of Israel
neither slumbers nor sleeps!

Adonai in your Guardian,

God is your protection at
your right hand.

The sun will not strike you by
day nor the moon by night.

Adonai will guard you from all harm--

Adonai will guard your soul,

you're going and your coming,

now and forever.

Night Prayer

Adonai, may it be Your will that
we lie down in peace and

rise up in peace. Let not our
thoughts, dreams, or daydreams

disturb us. Watch over all of us.

O Guardian of Israel, who neither
slumbers nor sleeps,

We entrust our spirits to You.
Thus as we go to sleep,

we put ourselves into Your safekeeping.

Grant us a night of rest. Let the
healing processes that

You have placed into our bodies
go about their work.

May we awaken in the morning,

refreshed and renewed to
face a new tomorrow.

Hear, O Israel, Adonai our
God, Adonai is One!

We praise You, Adonai, Whose
shelter of peace is spread over us,

over all Your people Israel, over every
creation, and over Jerusalem,

our spirits we commend to
You, our body too, and all we
prize; both when we sleep

and when we wake, You are with
us; we shall not fear, from the right,
from the left, from behind, from in
front, from below and from above
Your Divine Presence shelters us.

LINDA L LEWIS

Evening Shema

Hear, O Israel: Adonai is our God,
Adonai is One! Blessed is God's name;

His glorious kingdom is
for ever and ever!

And you shall love Adonai your God
with all your heart, with all your soul,

and with all your might.

And these words which I command
you this day shall be upon your heart;

teach them faithfully to your
children, speak of them in your

home and on your way, when you
lie down and when you rise up.

Bind them as a sign upon your hand;
let them be a symbol before your eyes.

Inscribe them on the doorposts of

your house and on your gates.

For Healing

Give ear, Adonai, to our prayer,
heed our plea for mercy. In time
of trouble we call to You,

for You will answer us.

When pain and fatigue are our
companions, let there be room
in our heart for strength.

When days and nights are filled
with darkness, let the light of
courage find its place.

Help us to endure the suffering
and dissolve the fear. Renew
within us the calm

spirit of peace.

Additional Blessings

Before Surgery

Adonai, You are with me in my moments of strength and of weakness.

You know the trembling of our hearts as the turning point draws near.

Grant wisdom and skill to the mind and hands of those who will operate

on me, and those who assist them. Grant that I may return to fullness of

life and wholeness of strength, not for my sake alone but for those about me.

Enable me to complete my days on earth with dignity and purpose. May I

awaken to know the breadth of Your healing power, now and evermore.

My spirit I commend to You, my body,

too, and all I prize; both when I sleep
and when I wake, You are
with me; I shall not fear.

Travelers Prayer

When leaving home for a short or long trip.

I like to say it anytime I
leave the house and

Sometimes I include it in
my daily prayers

anyway because Life is a journey every
moment of the day.

May it be Your will, Lord, our God
and the God of our ancestors,
that You lead us toward peace,
guide our footsteps toward peace,

and make us reach our
desired destination

for life, gladness, and peace.

(If one intends to return immediately,

one adds: and return us in peace).

May You rescue us from the hand of
every foe and ambush,

from robbers and wild
beasts on the trip,

and from all manner of punishments
that assemble to come to earth.

May You send blessing in
our handiwork,

and grant us grace, kindness,

and mercy in Your eyes
and in the eyes of

all who see us.

May You hear the sound of
our humble request

because You are God Who
hears prayer requests.

LINDA L LEWIS

Blessed are You, Lord,
Who hears prayer.

Food prayer

Blessed are You, Lord, Who
provides everything of its kind

For its own purpose and has given
us instruction on what is

good and acceptable for us
to eat and what is not.

We thank you for the food and
drink you have provided for

us to eat through Your wisdom,
creation, mercy and love

for us.

LINDA L LEWIS

Thank you so much for purchasing this book and I hope that it brings your soul comfort and peace in life always

Peace, Love and Happiness Always

Linda L Lewis

Printed in Great Britain
by Amazon